POEMS FOR AUTUMN

Selected by
Robert Hull

Illustrated by
Annabel Spenceley

Seasonal Poetry

Poems for Autumn
Poems for Spring
Poems for Summer
Poems for Winter

Series editor: Catherine Ellis
Designer: Ross George

First published in 1990 by
Wayland (Publishers) Ltd
61 Western Road, Hove
East Sussex BN3 1JD, England

**British Library Cataloguing in
Publication Data**
Poems for autumn.
1. Poetry in English, 1900–
–Anthologies
I. Hull, Robert II. Series
821.91208

ISBN 1–85210–882–7

Picture Acknowledgements

The publishers would like to thank the
following for allowing illustrations to be
reproduced in this book: Celtic Picture
Agency 41; Bruce Coleman *Cover*, (Hans
Reinhard) 5, (Hans Reinhard) 21, (Roger
Wilmshurst) 33, (John Shaw) 45; Eric & David
Hosking (George Hyde) 11; Frank Lane
Picture Agency (R Van Nostrand) 7, (M.
Nimmo) 17, (Peggy Heard) 29, (J. Bastable)
42; Topham Picture Library (Windridge) 13,
14, 18, 26, 38; Zefa (Palmer) 23, (Damm) 24,
31, 34, 37.

Acknowledgements

For permission to reprint copyright material
the publishers gratefully acknowledge the
following: Faber & Faber Ltd for 'October
Nights in My Cabin' from *Snowman Sniffles*
by N. M. Bodecker; the Estate of Robert Frost,
E. Connery Lathem and Jonathan Cape Ltd
for 'Gathering Leaves' from *The Collected
Poems of Robert Frost* edited by Edward
Connery Lathem; Faber & Faber Ltd for
'There Came a Day' from *Season Songs* by
Ted Hughes; the author and the Bodley Head
for 'Apple Song' from *The Spitfire on the
Northern Line* by Brian Jones, Chatto &
Windus/The Hogarth Press for 'Rowan Berry'
from *Collected Poems* by Norman MacCaig;
Faber & Faber Ltd for 'The Coming of the
Cold' from the *Collected Poems* of Theodore
Roethke; Collins Publishers for 'October'
from *Chicken Soup with Rice* by Maurice
Sendak; reprinted with permission of
Macmillan Publishing Company, 'Something
Told the Wild Geese', © 1934 Macmillan
renewed 1967 by Arthur S. Pederson;
Penguin Books for the two Haiku poems by
Masaoka Shiki trans. by Bownas and Thwaite
from *Penguin Book of Japanese Verse*; Wes
Magee for 'Tracey's Tree'; Brian Moses for
'Distributing the Harvest'; Ed Jenkins for
'Conker Raid'; Cynthia Mitchell for 'O
Witches and Wizards'; Matt Simpson for
'Autumn Haiku'; 'The Coming of the Cold',
copyright 1941 Theodore Roethke, used by
permission of Doubleday; 'October Nights in
My Cabin' reprinted with permission of
Margaret K. McElderry Books, copyright ©
1983 by N. M. Bodecker; Cadbury for 'The
Spell of a Witch' by Gillian Parker from
Cadbury's First Book of Children's Poetry.
While every effort has been made to secure
permission, in some cases it has proved
impossible to trace the copyright holders.

Typeset by Nicola Taylor, Wayland
Printed in Italy by G. Canale &
C.S.p.A., Turin
Bound in France by A.G.M.

Contents

Introduction

What does autumn make you think of? Blackberrying? Hallowe'en? Leaves falling? Coming in earlier because it gets dark sooner? Probably all of these things. And it means things like that to poets, too. It means feeling the sun getting chillier, sweeping leaves, going to harvest festivals, watching birds gobbling berries.

Poets do a lot of noticing. They notice insects getting slower. They notice the orchard trees 'sagging'. They STOP to look hard at things – until they see something they hadn't seen before. Have you ever played the game of staring at something until it reminds you of something else? You look hard at a tree-trunk and it becomes the skin of a dinosaur, or at a cauliflower until it reminds you of. . . ? That's always happening to poets.

That's how you can write autumn poems. Go outside to have a look at what's going on, get some conkers, pick some apples and blackberries, sweep up some leaves. Write. Read these poems again.

5

Something Told the Wild Geese

Something told the wild geese
  It was time to go.
Though the fields lay golden
  Something whispered — 'Snow'.
Leaves were green and stirring,
  Berries, lustre-glossed,
But beneath warm feathers
  Something cautioned — 'Frost'.
All the sagging orchards
  Steamed with amber spice,
But each wild breast stiffened
  At remembered ice.
Something told the wild geese
  It was time to fly —
Summer sun was on their wings,
  Winter in their cry.

RACHEL FIELD

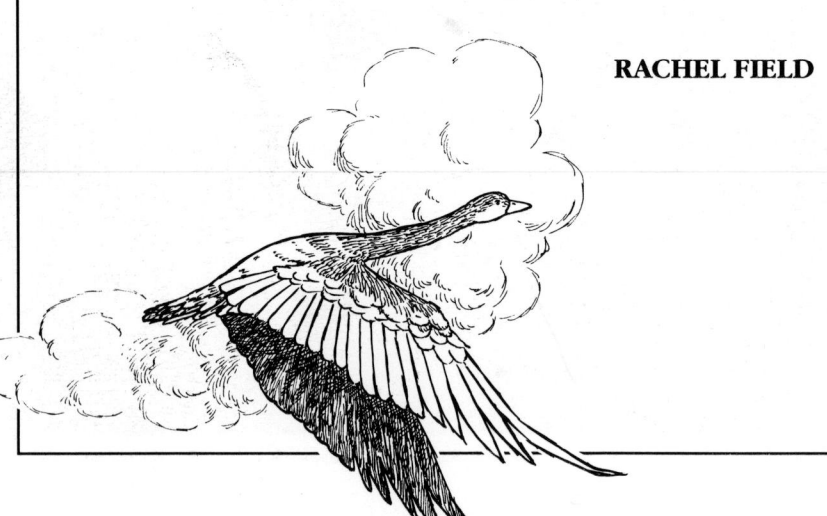

There Came a Day

There came a day that caught the summer
Wrung its neck
Plucked it
And ate it.

Now what shall I do with the trees?
The day said, the day said.
Strip them bare, strip them bare.
Let's see what is really there.

And what shall I do with the sun?
The day said, the day said.
Roll him away till he's cold and small.
He'll come back rested if he comes back at all.

And what shall I do with the birds?
The day said, the day said.
The birds I've frightened, let them flit,
I'll hang out pork for the brave tomtit.

And what shall I do with the seed?
The day said, the day said.
Bury it deep, see what it's worth.
See if it can stand the earth.

What shall I do with the people?
The day said, the day said.
Stuff them with apple and blackberry pie –
They'll love me then till the day they die.

There came this day and he was autumn.
His mouth was wide
And red as a sunset.
His tail was an icicle.

TED HUGHES

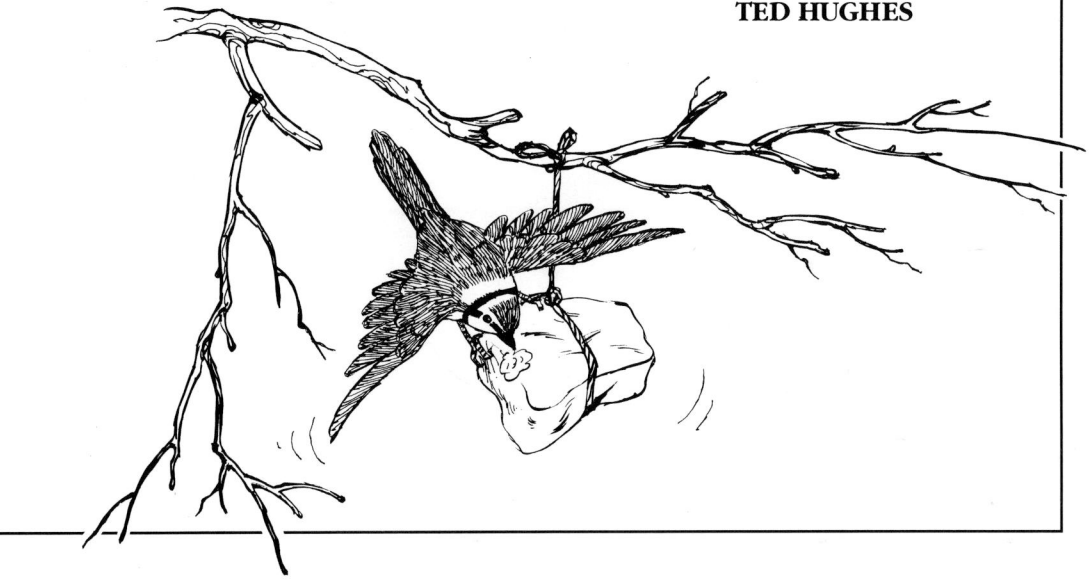

9

About Caterpillars

What about caterpillars?
Where do they crawl
when the stars say, 'Frost',
and the leaves say, 'Fall'?

Some go to sleep
in a white silk case
when the winds say, 'Blow!'
and the clouds say, 'Race!'

Some sleep in bags
of woven brown
or curl in a ball
when the year says, 'Frown'.

None has the least
little urge to know
what the world is like
when the sky says, 'Snow'.

AILEEN FISHER

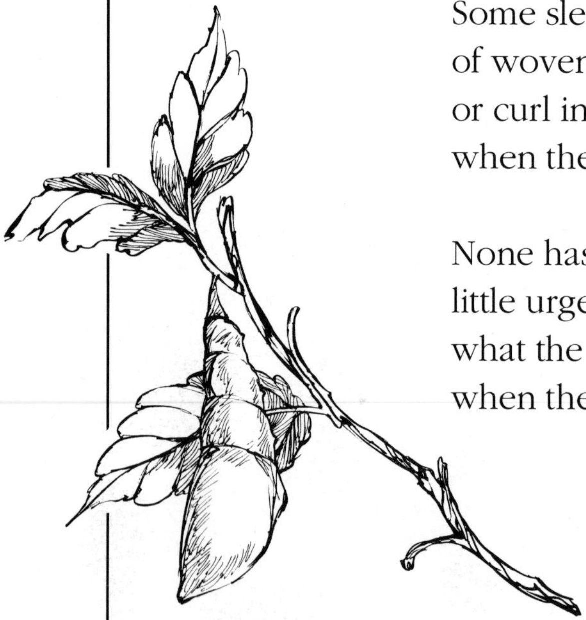

Lay Not Up

The bees
Sneeze and wheeze
    Scraping pollen and honey
From the lime trees:

The ants
Hurries and pants
    Storing up everything
They wants:

But the flies
Is wise
    When the cold weather comes
They dies.

L.W.G.

Apple Song

I am an apple
I swing on the tree
I have a sharpness
At the heart of me

And no sun at noonday
Brutal with heat
Can utterly tame me
And render me sweet

Don't eat me on picnics
At height of midsummer
With lettuce and radish
Tomatoes, cucumber

When your body is tanned
And your mind thick as cream
And all life a languorous
Strawberry dream

And when Autumn is stirred
By a spoon of a wind
And the clothes you are wearing
Seem suddenly thinned

And your walk through the orchard
Is vaguely beset
By currents of feeling –
Nostalgia, regret,

And you need an assurance
That December and June
Can be blended together,
Pluck me down. Eat me then.

BRIAN JONES

Rowan Berry

I'm at ease in my crimson cluster.
The tree blazes
with clusters of cousins –
my cluster's the main one and I
am the important berry in it.

Tomorrow, or tomorrow's tomorrow,
a flock of fieldfares
will gobble our whole generation.

I'm not troubled. My seed
will be shamelessly dropped
somewhere. And in the next years
after next year, I'll be a tree
swaying and swinging
with a genealogy of berries. I'll be
that fine thing, an ancestor.
I'll spread out my branches
for the guzzling fieldfares.

NORMAN MacCAIG

Tracey's Tree

Last year it was not there,
the sapling with purplish leaves
planted in our school grounds with care.
It's Tracey's tree, my friend who died,
and last year it was not there.

Tracey, the girl with long black hair
who, out playing one day, ran
across a main road for a dare.
The lorry struck her. Now a tree grows
and last year it was not there.

Through the classroom window I stare
and watch the sapling sway.
Soon its branches will stand bare.
It wears a forlorn and lonely look
and last year it was not there.

October's chill is in the air
and cold rain distorts my view.
I feel a sadness that's hard to bear.
The tree blurs, as if I've been crying,
and last year it was not there.

WES MAGEE

19

Theme in Yellow

I spot the hills
With yellow balls in autumn.
I light the prairie cornfields
Orange and tawny gold clusters
And I am called pumpkins.
On the last of October
When dusk is fallen
Children join hands
And circle round me
Singing ghost songs
And love to the harvest moon;
I am a jack-o'-lantern
With terrible teeth
And the children know
I am fooling.

CARL SANDBURG

The Spell of a Witch

I am making a magic spell,
With a toad and a goblin's yell.
A phantom's scream, a dragon's feather,
It smells as good as good as ever.
With frog's toes and lizard's legs,
I think I'll add some rotten eggs.
I scream and shout I moan and yell,
I've just found a snail's shell.
I'll add a pinch of dirty weather,
With a poison dragon's feather.
I stir my brew, I stir my brew,
Some for me and some for you.
Spooky, spooky dark and damp,
I met a wizard I met a tramp.
The wizard gave me a puppy dog's tail,
The tramp gave me a toad and a snail.
I stir my brew, I stir my brew,
Some for me and some for you.
I'll add some poison I'll add some blood,
I think it smells rather good.

GILLIAN PARKER (aged 9)

October Nights in My Cabin

Acorns drop
on my roof
all night,
each with a hard
little:
'Plonk!'

Raindrops drum
on my roof
all-right
like fingertips
over
my bunk.

Wild geese pass over
my roof
in flight,
the old, grey
travellers
honk!

There's a patter of feet
on my roof
that might
be a squirrel,
or chipmunk,
or skunk. . .

and acorns keep dropping
– or aren't they
quite
acorns, the things
that go:
'Bonk!'

but peanuts dropped
in the pale moonlight
from a fumble-nose
elephant's
trunk?

N. M. BODECKER

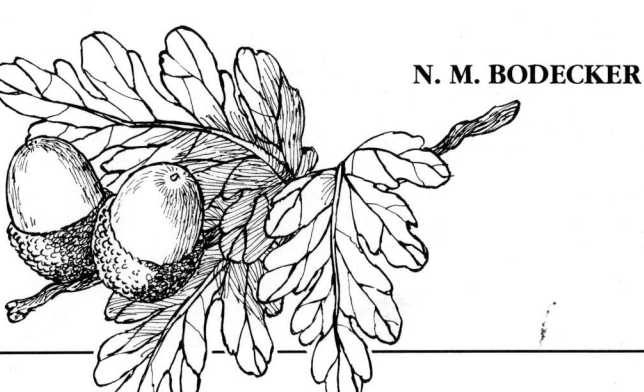

25

Distributing The Harvest (A Teacher's View)

We collapsed the tableau carefully,
passing it piece by piece to a class
of kids, arms held up to make their bids
for brussels, for solid & sensible spuds
to ballast the base of baskets,
while the eggs looked on from safe distance,
the tomatoes split their skins & sticky
apples slipped & rolled across the polished floor
to be challenged & captured & pushed
into bags, now swollen fat with harvest swag,
until all that remained were laidback marrows,
stout heroes of the garden patch.

Then burdens were lifted, shouldered &
shifted, till like some desert caravan of
Oriental kings with gifts, our harvest bearers
struggled out, towards the town, across the bridge.
Later we heard of casualties, someone's
cucumber spun under a car, while others on
the farthest run found no one home & hauled
it back or posted produce through letter flaps,
but then we knew nothing of that;
we heard instead, all afternoon, news of
successful missions & watched returning faces,
bright as harvest moons.

BRIAN MOSES

27

Crabapples

Sweeten these bitter wild crabapples, Illinois
October sun. The roots here came from the
wilderness, came before man came here. They
are bitter as the wild is bitter.

Give these crabapples your softening gold,
October sun, go through to the white wet
seeds inside and soften them black. Make
these bitter apples sweet. They want you, sun.

The drop and the fall, the drop and the fall,
the apples leaving the branches for the black
earth under, they know you from last year,
the year before last year, October sun.

CARL SANDBURG

October

In October
I'll be host
to witches, goblins
and a ghost.
I'll serve them
chicken soup
on toast.
Whoopy once
whoopy twice
whoopy chicken soup
with rice.

MAURICE SENDAK

Conker Raid

I was going for conkers
late at night –
after they'd turned off
the last light –

I crept down the garden
round about midnight –
there was a bit of a moon
but it wasn't bright –

and in next to no time
they were thumping round me,
all the best conkers
off that tree.

See, all this for me!
What's big about that?
Well just you try it,
you try it mate,

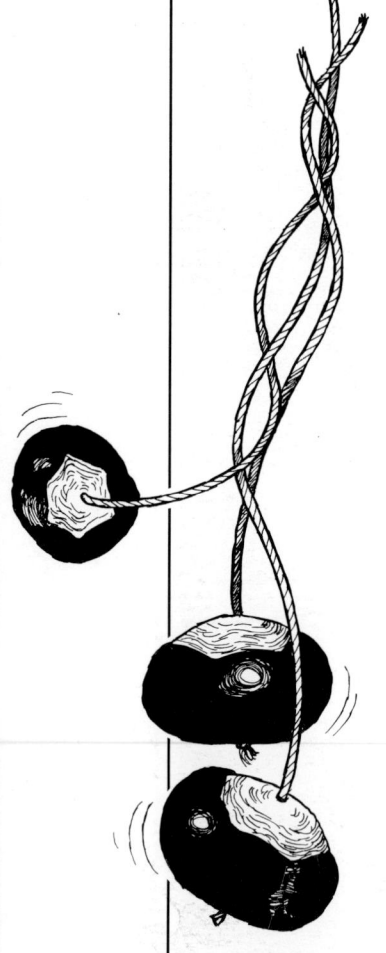

nicking the lot
secretly
from your own garden
when you're forty-three!

ED JENKINS

Gathering Leaves

Spades take up leaves
No better than spoons,
And bags full of leaves
Are light as balloons.

I make a great noise
Of rustling all day
Like rabbit and deer
Running away.

But the mountains I raise
Elude my embrace,
Flowing over my arms
And into my face.

I may load and unload
Again and again
Till I fill the whole shed,
And what have I then?

Next to nothing for weight,
And since they grew duller
From contact with earth,
Next to nothing for colour.

Next to nothing for use.
But a crop is a crop,
And who's to say where
The harvest shall stop?

ROBERT FROST

O Witches and Wizards

O witches and wizards, where have you been?
    We've been to a party for old Hallowe'en.

A Hallowe'en party! O what did you eat?
    Spiced turnip lanterns and hot cauldron treat.

And after the eating what games did you play?
    Old Spells, Hokey-Pokey, and Scare-Them-Away.

And after the game did you all dance together?
    We danced like the North wind in rough, stormy
        weather.

O witches and wizards, what else did you do?
    Ah, that is our secret. We cannot tell you.

CYNTHIA MITCHELL

The Roof Whirled Away by Winds

In the eighth moon of autumn, the wind howling viciously,
Three layers of thatch were whirled away from my roof.
The thatch flying over the river sprinkled the embankment
And some of it was entangled in the treetops,
And some whirled away and sank in the marshlands.
A swarm of small boys from South Village laughing at me because
    I am old and feeble.
They know they can rob me even in my face.
What effrontery! Stealing my thatch, taking it to the bamboo
    grove.
With parched lips and tongue I screamed at them – it was no
    use –
And so I came back sighing to my old place.
Then the wind fell and the clouds were inky black,
The autumn sky a web of darkness, stretching toward the dusk,
And my old cotton quilt was as cold as iron,
And my darling son tossed in his sleep, bare feet tearing
    through the blanket,
And the rain dripped through the roof, and there was no dry
    place on the bed.
Like strings of wax the rain fell, unending.
After all these disasters of war, I have had little sleep or rest.
When will this long night of drizzle come to an end?

TU FU

39

A Sheep Fair

The day arrives of the autumn fair,
  And torrents fall,
Though sheep in throngs are gathered there,
  Ten thousand all,
Sodden, with hurdles round them reared:
And, lot by lot, the pens are cleared,
And the auctioneer wrings out his beard,
And wipes his book, bedrenched and smeared,
And rakes the rain from his face with the edge of his hand,
  As torrents fall.

The wool of the ewes is like a sponge
  With the daylong rain:
Jammed tight, to turn, or lie, or lunge,
  They strive in vain.
Their horns are as soft as finger-nails,
Their shepherds reek against the rails,
The tied dogs soak with tucked-in tails,
The buyers' hat-brims fill like pails,
Which spill small cascades when they shift their stand
  In the daylong rain.

THOMAS HARDY

Autumn Haiku

This Way Winter! say
a robin's arrow-tracks on
the garden's first snow.

MATT SIMPSON

He washes his horse
With the setting sun
In the autumn sea.

MASAOKA SHIKI

A snake falls
From the high stone wall:
Fierce autumn gale.

MASAOKA SHIKI

The Coming of the Cold

The ribs of leaves lie in the dust,
The beak of frost has picked the bough,
The briar bears its thorn, and drought
Has left its ravage on the field.
The season's wreckage lies about,
Late autumn fruit is rotted now.
All shade is lean, the antic branch
Jerks skyward at the touch of wind,
Dense trees no longer hold the light,
The hedge and orchard grove are thinned.
The dank bark dries beneath the sun,
The last of harvesting is done.
All things are brought to barn and fold
The oak leaves strain to be unbound,
The sky turns dark, the year grows old,
The buds draw in before the cold.

THEODORE ROETHKE

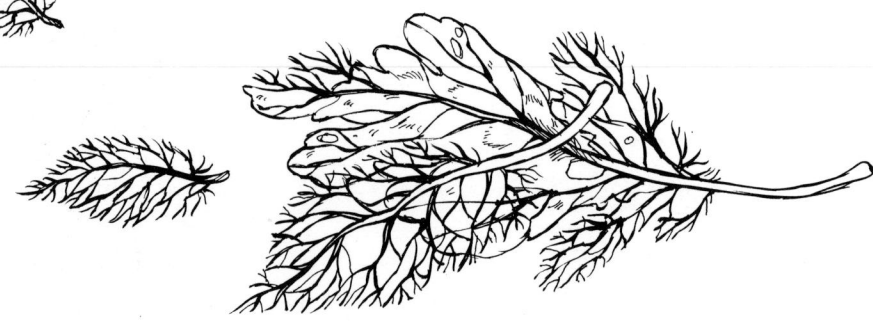

Biographies

N. M. Bodecker was born in Denmark, and now lives in the USA. He spent his early life painting and drawing, then started to write at about twenty. He has three sons and lives in New Hampshire in an old haunted house.

Rachel Field (1894–1942) was an American writer. She was born in New York, then lived in Massachusetts. She wrote lots of children's poetry and stories, and novels for adults.

Aileen Fisher is best known for *In the Woods, in the Meadow, in the Sky*, a poetry collection published in 1965.

Robert Frost (1874–1963) is one of the most famous American poets of this century. He was born in California, and later lived on a farm in Vermont. Although he did not write books especially for children, many of his poems are children's favourites.

Tu Fu is one of the most famous Chinese poets. He lived more than a thousand years ago, from AD 712 to 770, and wrote hundreds of poems.

Thomas Hardy (1840–1928) was a famous novelist and poet, who lived nearly all his long life in Dorset. He is one of the greatest English poets.

Ted Hughes was born in Yorkshire. In 1984 he was made Poet Laureate. He has written many books for adults and for children. One of the best known for children is *Season Songs*.

Ed Jenkins was born in Lancashire. He runs poetry workshops and poetry readings for children in schools, and he writes poetry for children.

Brian Jones was born in London, and now lives in Kent. He has published books of poems for children and adults, and has received many awards.

Norman MacCaig was born in 1910 in Edinburgh. He writes a great deal about Scotland, and has published many collections of poetry.

Wes Magee lives in Yorkshire. He is a full-time writer who started writing for adults and went on to write books for children. A recent one is *Morning Break*, voted one of the best children's books of 1989.

Cynthia Mitchell lives in Yorkshire, where she used to be deputy head of an infants' school. She has written three books of verse for children. She visits schools with her poems, and likes to get children to skip and dance and be active with her poems, as you might guess from the title of one book: *Hopalong Happily*.

Brian Moses was a teacher, and is now a freelance writer living in Sussex. He visits schools doing writing workshops and performances. Many of his poems for children have been published in anthologies, and his collection *Leave Your Teddy Behind* was published in 1988.

Theodore Roethke (1908–1963) was born in Saginaw. After leaving Chicago he taught English at several colleges in the USA. His poems for children are in a book called *I Am! Says the Lamb!*

Carl Sandburg (1878–1967) was an American writer. He wrote many stories and poems for children. They are collected in a beautiful book called *The Sandburg Treasury*.

Maurice Sendak is best known as an illustrator of many children's books, such as the famous *Where the Wild Things Are*, voted the best picture book of 1963 in the USA. He was born in Brooklyn in 1928, and started making books with his brother Jack when they were both quite young.

Masaoka Shiki (1867–1902) was a Japanese writer of haiku. Haiku are three-line poems which have been popular in Japan for many centuries. Shiki used to advise his pupils to 'be natural' and try for 'real pictures' when writing poetry.

Matt Simpson started writing for children only fairly recently. His latest book of poems for adults is called *An Elegy for the Galosherman*. He lives in Liverpool, where he lectures in English, and visits schools to read his poetry.

Index of first lines